Our Country's Holidays/
Las fiestas de nuestra nación

Flag Day/
Día de la Bandera
by/por Sheri Dean

Reading consultant/Consultora de lectura:
Susan Nations, M.Ed.,
author/literacy coach/consultant in literacy development
autora/tutora de alfabetización/
consultora de desarrollo de la lectura

Please visit our web site at: www.garethstevens.com
For a free color catalog describing our list of high-quality books,
call 1-800-542-2595 (USA) or 1-800-387-3178 (Canada).

Library of Congress Cataloging-in-Publication Data available upon request from publisher.
Fax (414) 336-0157 for the attention of the Publishing Records Department.

ISBN-10: 0-8368-6518-9 (lib. bdg.)
ISBN-13: 978-0-8368-6518-9 (lib. bdg.)
ISBN-10: 0-8368-6525-1 (softcover)
ISBN-13: 978-0-8368-6525-7 (softcover)

This edition first published in 2006 by
Weekly Reader® Early Learning Library
A Member of the WRC Media Family of Companies
330 West Olive Street, Suite 100
Milwaukee, WI 53212 USA

Copyright © 2006 by Weekly Reader® Early Learning Library

Managing editor: Valerie J. Weber
Art direction: Tammy West
Cover design and page layout: Kami Strunsee
Picture research: Cisley Celmer
Translators: Tatiana Acosta and Guillermo Gutiérrez

Picture credits: Cover, © White Cross Productions/Getty Images; p. 5 © Gary Randall/Getty Images;
p. 7 © Gary Conner/PhotoEdit; p. 9 © Joel Sartore/National Geographic Image Collection; p. 11
© Stephen Simpson/Getty Images; p. 13 © Tom Carter/PhotoEdit; p. 15 © Tony Freeman/PhotoEdit;
p. 17 © Skjold Photographs; p. 19 © Gibson Stock Photography; p. 21 © Lilly Dong/Getty Images

Printed in the United States of America

2 3 4 5 6 7 8 9 10 09 08 07

Note to Educators and Parents

Reading is such an exciting adventure for young children! They are beginning to integrate their oral language skills with written language. To encourage children along the path to early literacy, books must be colorful, engaging, and interesting; they should invite the young reader to explore both the print and the pictures.

In *Our Country's Holidays*, children learn how the holidays they celebrate in their families and communities are observed across our nation. Using lively photographs and simple prose, each title explores a different national holiday and explains why it is significant.

Each book is specially designed to support the young reader in the reading process. The familiar topics are appealing to young children and invite them to read — and reread — again and again. The full-color photographs and enhanced text further support the student during the reading process.

In addition to serving as wonderful picture books in schools, libraries, homes, and other places where children learn to love reading, these books are specifically intended to be read within an instructional guided reading group. This small group setting allows beginning readers to work with a fluent adult model as they make meaning from the text. After children develop fluency with the text and content, the book can be read independently. Children and adults alike will find these books supportive, engaging, and fun!

— Susan Nations, M.Ed., author, literacy coach,
and consultant in literacy development

Nota para los maestros y los padres

¡Leer es una aventura tan emocionante para los niños pequeños! A esta edad están comenzando a integrar su manejo del lenguaje oral con el lenguaje escrito. Para animar a los niños en el camino de la lectura incipiente, los libros deben ser coloridos, estimulantes e interesantes; deben invitar a los jóvenes lectores a explorar la letra impresa y las ilustraciones.

Con la serie *Las fiestas de nuestra nación* los jóvenes lectores aprenderán que las fiestas que sus familias y sus comunidades celebran son días especiales en todo el país. Mediante vistosas fotografías y textos sencillos, cada libro explora una fiesta nacional diferente y explica por qué es importante.

Cada libro está especialmente diseñado para ayudar a los jóvenes lectores en el proceso de lectura. Los temas familiares llaman la atención de los niños y los invitan a leer — y releer — una y otra vez. Las fotografías a todo color y el tamaño de la letra ayudan aún más al estudiante en el proceso de lectura.

Además de servir como maravillosos libros ilustrados en escuelas, bibliotecas, hogares y otros lugares donde los niños aprenden a amar la lectura, estos libros han sido especialmente concebidos para ser leídos en un grupo de lectura guiada. Este contexto permite que los lectores incipientes trabajen con un adulto que domina la lectura mientras van determinando el significado del texto. Una vez que los niños dominan el texto y el contenido, el libro puede ser leído de manera independiente. ¡Estos libros les resultarán útiles, estimulantes y divertidos a niños y a adultos por igual!

— Susan Nations, M.Ed., autora/tutora de alfabetización/
consultora de desarrollo de la lectura

Flag Day is the birthday of our flag!

—— —— —— —— —— —— —— —— —— —— —— —— ——

¡El Día de la Bandera es el cumpleaños de nuestra bandera!

4

5

Every country has a flag. Our flag stands for the United States of America.

Todos los países tienen una bandera. Nuestra bandera representa a Estados Unidos de América.

6

Red, white, and blue are the special colors of our flag. Fifty stars and thirteen stripes are on our flag.

Rojo, blanco y azul son los colores de nuestra bandera. En nuestra bandera hay cincuenta estrellas y trece barras.

8

Flag Day is always on June 14. Many people fly an American flag on this day.

- -

El Día de la Bandera es siempre el 14 de junio. Ese día, muchas personas izan una bandera de Estados Unidos.

On Flag Day, Americans honor their flag and their country. Some people watch parades.

El Día de la Bandera, los estadounidenses honran a su país y su bandera. Algunos van a ver los desfiles.

13

There are special rules about caring for the flag. We fold our worn flags and put them away. New flags go up.

━ ━ ━ ━ ━ ━ ━ ━ ━ ━ ━ ━ ━ ━ ━ ━ ━

Hay reglas especiales para tratar la bandera. Doblamos las banderas desgastadas y las guardamos. Se ponen banderas nuevas.

14

The flag should never touch the ground.

La bandera nunca debe tocar el suelo.

17

Our flag should always fly higher than any other flag around it.

Nuestra bandera siempre debe colocarse más alta que cualquier otra bandera.

On Flag Day, we put out our flag. We are proud to be Americans!

-- -- -- -- -- -- -- -- -- -- -- -- -- -- --

El Día de la Bandera, sacamos nuestra bandera. ¡Estamos orgullosos de ser estadounidenses!

21

Glossary

American — a person from the United States of America

country — the land that forms a nation

honor — to show respect

proud — to be very pleased about something

Glosario

estadounidense — persona de Estados Unidos de América

honrar — mostrar respeto

orgulloso — muy complacido

país — territorio que forma una nación

For More Information/ Más información

Books

Flag Day. National Holidays (series). Mari C. Schuh (Pebble Books)

What Freedom Means to Me: A Flag Day Story. Heather French Henry (Cubbie Blue Publishing)

Libros

Bandera. Símbolos de libertad (series). Tristan Boyer Binns (Sagebrush)

La bandera que amamos/The Flag We Love. Pam Muñoz Ryan (Sagebrush)

Web Sites/Páginas web

Betsy Ross Home Page
Página de Betsy Ross
www.ushistory.org/betsy/flagpics.html
Read about the different flags the United States has used throughout its history.
Conoce las diferentes banderas de Estados Unidos a lo largo de la historia.

Index

Índice

About the Author

Sheri Dean is a school librarian in Milwaukee, Wisconsin. She was an elementary school teacher for fourteen years. She enjoys introducing books and information to curious children and adults.

Información sobre la autora

Sheri Dean trabaja como bibliotecaria en Milwaukee, Wisconsin. Durante catorce años, fue maestra de primaria. A Sheri le gusta proporcionar información y libros novedosos a niños y adultos con ganas de aprender.